SUPERIOR PACKETS

SUPERIOR PACKETS

THREE BOOKS BY

SUSIE TIMMONS

WAVE BOOKS   SEATTLE AND NEW YORK

PUBLISHED BY WAVE BOOKS

WWW.WAVEPOETRY.COM

WAVE BOOKS TITLES ARE DISTRIBUTED TO THE TRADE BY

CONSORTIUM BOOK SALES AND DISTRIBUTION

PHONE: 800-283-3572 / SAN 631-760X

LIBRARY OF CONGRESS CATALOGING-IN-PUBLICATION DATA

TIMMONS, SUSIE.

[POEMS. SELECTIONS]

SUPERIOR PACKETS / SUSIE TIMMONS. — FIRST EDITION.

PAGES ; CM

ISBN 978-1-940696-05-8 (HARDCOVER) — ISBN 978-1-940696-06-5 (SOFTCOVER)

I. TITLE.

PS3570.I462A6 2015

811'.54—DC23

2014020733

DESIGNED AND COMPOSED BY QUEMADURA

PRINTED IN THE UNITED STATES OF AMERICA

9   8   7   6   5   4   3   2   1

FIRST EDITION

HOG WILD (1979)

LOCKED FROM THE OUTSIDE (1990)

THE NEW OLD PAINT (2010)

ON THE DAILY MONUMENT

CHICKADEES IN THE SNOW

HOG WILD

1979

THE SPANISH HARPS

We are the Spanish Harps,
and this is our salute to you.
We are the Spanish Harps,
We certainly hope you like us.
We are the Spanish Harps,
Vwing, Vwing, Vwing.

ASIAN ROBE

Your mind is like a parachute; it works best when it is open.
or vice versa
or not at all
better to be floating upward
than a leaf in the Fall
upward I woke up
on Tuesday
planted firmly
the calendar forgotten
the day off
the air was humming
and across the way
some radio
some lady
could be heard some
clinking washing dishes
thinking heat and I got up
Eureka I am rich
I have two new pairs of shoes
just in time for Spring
they're tapping in time
with spring
even last Saturday
cold and rainy
the trees in the park
were unmistakably
pale green
what can I say to that
except that
that's what I call progress
Eureka I'm rich!
and my asian robe has
opened to disclose
smooth blue air
with clouds and violins, humming

STRETCHED HOMEWARD

You, as useful
as a silk hat
in a hurricane
few things are

clear as the coast
is on before me
flags wave over
the Club Hibiscus

sailboats arrive
filled with lovers
with wings
that fill

chronic blue skies
stretched homeward
more favorable
than billowing

or otherwise
favored clouds
and safe return
so lovely a night

BIG TIME

The past lies densely in folds
sliding loose to feel I'd slept a minute
a terrific minute, streamly hoop of hours
or strong tidings driving ashore no doubt
a shawl; the spotted object on the ground
fallen from the shoulders of a woman standing
near and so constant.

GOD IS LOVE

Boon companions hung lanterns
in tall palms on a reef, and
when ships came crashing in
looted them.
God is love, angel baby
and morning star
dream city of romance, deft shadings,
Normandy in a bathing suit.
I haven't any religion
but I thought what we did
the other night was not wrong.
Precious had a colt
which Betty promptly named
sugar sweetheart honey darling.

CLOTHESLINE BALLET

Cigarettes, cold beers
classic fixtures
what we need here is a
lesson we learned
a color scheme
plus recalls, smithereens
true green is very green
almost black as broken records
dark lights are still
on a gleaming beauty's leg
almost as black, long shinned
where each room in this head has
a where did you get it bathrobe
of pale sky striped pink
but spaced out like the olden days.
Serpentine
vinyl book covers
stepping out of the subway
into a change of weather
teetering on weak ankles
I used to think by force of will
get rid of linoleum under stove
plaster by tub, spackle all holes
apertures, get brillos, toilet paper
floors walls ceilings pipes radiators
but I have fallen by the wayside,
not the sidewalk but the footaway.
What shall we say shall we call it
African Ripple—Clothesline Ballet
Alligator Crawl—Viper's Drag
these above were the songs that played
and Softer than Velvet was the night.
While we were asleep the air was busy
while he was asleep we were busy

while we were busy we forgot the air
forget about me and I'll die,
not really, but
my body it needs resting now
and arm in arm with arm
the part in my hair has resurfaced
so get yourself what you need
smile smile smile
and believe I
believe I've
been doing this for years
from neglect, density equals intensity
like a maze and I am a master boatsman
fading to the atmospheric daytime
Thanks for the pointer
squadrons of coffee, a 7up and
damp chill, plumbing, reflection;
A crescent of broken mirror
ill advised by a stranger
that knows
a failure in the reflecting world
is dissolved.
Thud! Ouish!
stars flopping on the sands.
Lights flash behind body to face off
waiting, whistling anxious trucks
if you're really freaking out you know
you can figure something out, you know?
It should all be happening at once by now.
Raining is all I can think of,
a terrible matinee of downpour
it won't ever stop maybe not.
In the meantime, the African map
in the bathroom ripples and crawls
is burning up, like on Bonanza
in my head of course.
And it does rain.

It's not a big chair.
Note clock: five to seven
I'm dragging this thing in and out
because faith is you, young and compliant
it's some mysterious something
an area of soaring skyscrapers
plus modern style.
That's how I enjoy distance
nights bolted together moistly.
Lafayette, empire, desolate
of people all poured away
and still pouring secretly away.
Streetlights wreathed in fog, the lights
flattened to ribbons in the street
and shining Vacancy on Vacancy off
back to school, can't wash my sweaters
because traffic punctuated, perforated
every twenty minutes and summarized
the situation.
Lady on train, David is my secret drum
my revolution rowboat, my secret drum.
Though the talks are in trouble
and strikes are in store
though the plain has been stormed
it's like lightning striking again
and again and again and again, a classic.
Forty years ago I stood before this river,
this house, this fern, this leopard
and I am proud to say I restored.

BRIGHT WALLS

I dived into the grass
when people go by
in country fresh cars
once I knew them but
I don't know them.
I changed my job and now
I don't see you anymore.
You came this far
what do you want from me?
You lied by saying love
was life's greatest reward
but there's no reward
for love in this life
but bright walls
one after the other.
I was mistaken and caused
myself to be unavailable
to no avail, rain falls
like all the time before.
I am no pretty little thing
my mind is no athlete either
who could race downstairs
forward to events
say hello to forty people
people in need of detail

I prefer my kitchen table

I believe you've seen it

standing there.

Isn't it fortunate

we have that much in common?

SCABBY LEGS

First it snowed
then the sun came out

first it snowed
then the sun came out

nature is a wondrous cycle
nature is a truly wondrous cycle

how much water is in the air
how much sun and heat is in the air
you and I like to breathe?

that is the weather
I love to talk about

Yes, I love to talk about the weather

the smiling sun goes down
behind a frowning cloud

little jets stream into the smiling sun
above our tenth street penthouse.

You feel constructive

but can't do anything about it

hat and convention

hand in hand

hardy har

penny rolls

a high quality

brown bottle

of rose, blue

brush and candy

busy with pencils

and here comes the steam

red hot

and sickly as an olive

flexible drift

" click "

go the pencils

extraordinaire

distracting

my close me is

nearly

and right to be

in my hand

palm or tree

all the way up

from the ground floor

brilliantly varied

those colors never run out.

Here it is another way:

my desk in the causeway

feels like a test

and this is the answer to

the essay question.

Peppers curve over a scarf

of arrows and cambric dots.

Covered wagon

tumbling clouds

spill over the brink

red car, cigar

dark trees, yellow halls

with stencils on them

dogs on every step

soaring skyscrapers

floor 16, elevator ping

marching with newspaper

millions, under their arm

rubble

blondes in rubble

in anklets

I live my life like a

hula hoop, I wish.

Not blond, not bad

leaves down now,

shades

down, up.

One more time

coming indoors

it's cool as a cucumber

outdoors it's sunny and tan.

In my house, new vistas

terrible howls

as the lunatic on the top floor

hurls cat chow at my window.

In my house there's fur

and the green forest trees

beige colored jar

copper pennies

red paper   penny rolls.

Fresh curbs, stricken

in the gravelly morning

lotion and a box of dolls

Don't be so bitter when

I point out the nifty

dynamic lights curving

over the gas pumps, it's

deflating and disturbing.

Oh fell swoop, Flexible Flyer

leaning outside the five and dime.

Two tone pink tiles

black grout, soiled pale

sneakers, black jeans

and the electronic towel.

Precise mercury

you are the striking chord

that stands forward and

pulls the song along,

out of the radio

into my head

whence I cast it out

into the air whistling.

I like you because you

sleep in the forest floor.

Don't be all electrical

overloaded

it's the law, it saves lives

and certainly work must be done.

You go and you go,

tough getting started

when once you do you go and go.

Getting go, white pants pushing past

celadon chair. So much

I want to tell you how

really articulate I am in percents.

A closure on the wall

gently herds herds his sheep.

As a child, who wouldn't think

the black one was a gorilla

bringing up the rear?

Rain is falling on this steep boat

and turning into mothballs.

Epic winter is upon us

known in my region

as the long tunnel.

A good thing to do is dream

of violence with your neighbor.

Terriers dot the sky blue lines

of your infancy. The lines

of the world shift and change,

I get hysterical and my insides

seem to be a vapor.

You and me against the oyster

plaids, stripes, for I am

deeper than the Chile-Peru trench

and higher than the Andean Accordian

and steeper than this boat,

and it is in that fashion I

slide over or under.

Here is a bit of my history:

everything to me was an entity

I named them friend or enemy

Freight trains crossing

Grosse Point Rd. taught me to be

a fast reader.

These trains had snow frosting
their tops in the chirping spring.
Thunderstorms crashed along
the high tension wires
sending my grandmother
drunk, down the stairs.
The wires buzzed when the weather
was humid along the Milwaukee Road.
An obscure retarded child named Alan
raced up the dead end sideways,
waved his arms frantically at
every passing train.
I woke up one morning in New Jersey
and all the birds were singing
in unison, very organized
like an opera.
After a certain point
my life becomes my life.
Now it's nighttime in your bed
warm and you're awake
awake, the moon is string beaning
across the low heavens like
sliced melon, or dishware, maybe
you've seen it, you know what I mean:
everything is so utterly peaceful
you're going wild.
What you mean is

I just wanted to come home

sit down before the TV so

why be mad at me?

That's what you mean

the way you feel

what you mean

my idea.

Nothing by it, but

floating skirts in the wind

this beautiful Japanese Pearl Queen

explicitly is what is meant.

You like to see what you might find,

which often turns out to be a big

nothing.

Why try to keep it out?

Green River, Shoppers Special

the time has come to turn on the

sign, to turn on the record,

to generate small hearts who float

away from the Victrola, to pause and then

"pop" "pop" "pop" "pop"

in air over melancholy head.

This should keep you satisfied

up to one minute ago.

KEEP ON GOING

Keep on going, old slappy head.
A question in the west
zealot studies
excitable, disastrous
very trembling, goodness
Better Not.   How youthful
the nocturn mumbling
kiss kiss outdoors like a peony,
Keep on going old slappy head.

FINITY

There's nothing
a ghost hates
more than complaining
amorphous or crystalline
substance in solution
the ocean
was full of boats
and there were lots
of old people
if only I could tell
of the warmth
of our island
it wasn't much
but what it was
was generous
a charmed individual
in the brilliant afternoon
the trees stirring
the sky
the weather
so bright as to be disturbing
the muddy backyards of
springtime
notwithstanding
the fabulous concept
of four wheel drive
a popular stroll
in the public domain
emphasis
falling like oaken shade
down elusive avenues
on two folding chairs
ambiguously symbolic
yet to be indelicate
alert and watchful
unfinished or better
as ever

MY MEMORY

It is interesting, the way you

incorporate the sputtering scaffold.

I'm not dumb, but my memory is

under a mountain, blue-veined, immense.

It is possible that later you will

stroke my wing beneath the arbor.

Your limbs clamor to reach the border

although distant, arching, in the meantime.

OBIT

A man is dead, he was antique
his death was antique
in minor modes, he certified
his speech as gasoline
his name was Mr. Bone
all cellular
world & water
he was a monument to heat
a question, a proof
an effect
spectral notion, notation
his region was the first
part to assert focus
firmly on motion of distrust
love, and sizzling terrain
obscured by machinery moths.

IRON FAN

Small Garden
Faulty Pen
Dated Clothing
Mighty Sparrow
Squeaking Cart
Hot Breeze
Tormented Individual

Across from this small garden,
and written with a faulty pen
I note the dated clothing I wear
I note the song of the mighty sparrow
I hear the sing song of a squeaking wheelcart
in the hot breeze I am a tormented individual
flagging myself with an iron fan.

BILL SENT: A COMET

Bill sent
Bill sent the message
Bill sent the message to Harry at once.

Pyramids: inside he was thinking
he just might live to be forever.

One cannot
One can discover
much of what it
the message said.

(A raincoat for a movie star)

Whether it was
Whether it was written or oral
or written on coral
angry or dismayed

begged asked demanded.
Harry should fulfil his promises.
And should make the message
fit his own version of the promises.

He could hardly
He could believe what had transpired.
And wanted it himself,
it was nothing irrevocable.

adamant.
offered.
The excuse appeared
and later chronicled.

Those which he had,
making the promises,
his failure to keep them
they proved impossible to keep.

Then, accord
sweetly sent a second.
Will You Marry My Daughter?
This is one of the strangest reports!

The whole business is intriguing,
It was.

ODD AND EVEN

The world began, and so
rise and scatter
Smoke untwist
and vanish away
wax and wane—
early in the morning
bearing women, a angel
proclaim the glad
this is the day
the day has made.

PORTO BELLO

On Saturday night
gold miners courted their girls
by sprinkling gold dust in their hair.

If you have two
lizards tattooed on your neck
it signifies sleeping with the one desired.

At this moment
a pyramid of bullets
circles our globe slightly North of the equator.

Some customers
want opium, but all
an American Sailor wants is a cigarette.

LOCKED
FROM THE
OUTSIDE

1990

WHERE I LEFT OFF

If pillows were people they'd always be sleeping

in my library book there's a man playing a bug

for his musical instrument

pillows and speckled navy enamel cup

you can't even wave

good eye

an ochre

pyramid, big chief notebooks

pencils neatly sharpened, smokestacks

is turn, into, or ones with fire on their tip all night

with the fire coming in.

camisole. universe walking past Veselka

down Ninth Street, east, rainy January, 11 p.m.

jackals howling

translucent bottle containing disc preener

sable, lace caps

letters and stamps

the woodwork expels an example

flying for humans, talking animals, reading minds

I can't believe the bell here,

sick analog

ten flawless lines

the coast is a dream

at her bath and stuck gently on her forehead

CORRESPONDENCE

Dear thousand John

                        I am writing

you only sent me, you move often.

Well How

the country life

         1921

        *

all the 'chickens'

the scandal of seventh street

                 Joe Morgan is my bodyguard

Otto brough his girl a wedding ring

for 12.00

or 72.00

            we had a stake cake and coffey.

and a big cigar

                 Saturday afternoon, of course

say Kid the water was   fine

She is just like Josie, shes got that NO

well bey hect   I met them about 20 minutes to 8

and I had to go away to a show,   in a new motorcycle

up B'way

Bristol's

stand in her doorway and muzzle her

SWISS CHARD

frenzied mobs
loot the great
house

Epingles
De Fantaisie

the greed of
organization man

memories of Alaska
Take
a
Drive to
Scarsdale

Bathroom at
Loews Astor Plaza

swiss chard
Mary Tyler Moore
kissing
James Garner

way back when
threaded through
I resign
I gesture
hands up, palms out
shudder, so what

Sirens through the August night

learn to play
pipeline on a pieplate

"Twot Hole
That's it nothing
else!"

one wish:
world peace

VISION ADORNED WITH SUCKER

grey and white oilcloth, two cathedrals

separated by a tidal creek

or man-made chemical drainage ditch, puddle

adorning

this dismal vignette

an assortment of wrenches

floating hither and yon, with a real

lollipop stuck right onto the plastic.

THE GLASS

Rippling

notion

5 taxis

Formica

on Tintern Abbey

morose.

alert

for a difference

the ruler poised at desk's edge

glowing embers

from a gas explosion

ragged curtains fluttering

sliding door blown out

christmas decorations scattered all over the yard

a coal mine in Utah

fire one mile into the mine

they've been in there 26 hours and it doesn't

their chance of survival is bad.

Webb Pierce.   When I look at the dirty little bed

and nothing blooming.

FIRST

back porch

spray exploding
from hose
onto clay flowerpots
stacked up
on special
area over
steps to cellar

he is the glue
that holds us together

family

plant life

the theater of my family
was on fire; by sunup
nothing was left but concrete stairways

milkbox
stroganoff
things to work:
lock & key
hose

some of the people on
their way to the camp
offered to take me with them

examples of lo riders:

pals

sittin in low wall
concrete wall

monkeys, lions
comprehensive
list of all the animals
mosquitoes, LEECHES

whoop of a hyena
a small boy with a paddle
sat perched on the back of a log

early July morning of one particular year
my birthday.

an interior of crushed velvet
red or black—velvet all over

horse chestnut

with snow flurries
winter   fall

ROMAN PICNIC

The clouds are very large, very threatening, wouldn't
you say?

Now in New York, we know it's pouring.

Here, waiting for the downpour
at a green picnic table, blue green
the color of tomato sticks
or windowsills in Pittsburgh.

The table is slanting, tilted
off in the weeds of an untended
vegetable garden.   Evening Primrose.

I realized this minute swallows
are about swallowing, I never connected
the two before.

SUNDAY IS

sunday is a man's office
in minutes
a girl's secret life
(scale up)

thank you I promised awkwardly

I guess they live completely under the ground plunger

next to the sponge leaning up against the lightbulb

attached at the roots, almost blind.

WITCH HAZEL

if only to remember

what feels like

room for improvement

do everyday

weary of fantasies

fear of work

fear of "ernesto"

witch hazel is quite cool,

you can brush your teeth with witch hazel you know.

how did they recognize he's good?

well he remember was an extremely handsome charming young man.

FOR EILEEN

after speaking with you on the phone this morning

went out and stood in the snow

waiting for the bus to school.   to work

Huge perfect snowflakes stuck to my mittens

    to my gloves

blue jay was shrieking in one of those trees nearby

street sweeper passed

blue jay vanished

ripples and cloudy sky in black puddle

winter won't be here forever, but

I don't feel like I want to tell myself a lot of

lies about what's going to happen when spring comes

life's going too fast, and with all this

recent gazing backward I wish time would slow down

It was just back then, recently, there's no division

between my present and my childhood

I've always been myself, same as I was

After talking to you I felt better, did you feel awful?

To be large and happy like   the sun

with ne'er a dread nor worry!

CRAMPS ARE LIKE GOATS

children who perform with a disease
     cloddity
are escaping.   They are wearing
     housepants.

SPRING CLASSICS

The thin actress
ripped the medal from Mother's neck.

She gathered up her telegrams and
set them apart.

More emeralds.　　I wish I were here
I wish though that I were you.

POEM

cause I want crinkled foil and water

CHAUCER   and rose petals, are additionally desirable

SHAKESPEARE   and also able to look over at

SPENSER   shadows on lawn of

MILTON   stately Arkansas statehood.

BLAKE

KEATS

SWIFT

SENSITIVE DIVIDER

The time has come for me to take my message to the pale swamp

for me to sit talking by myself

for extrapolating whatever exists
within my narrow frame of vision

whatever happens, we agree on one thing—
transportation wields employment

the usual leaders are singularly divided
                                    a singular device
            cranks and whines its way into the guidelines

I come ecstatic, realistic
Foundation picture
        one million one hundred and seventy thousand
Indian maidens, or a latitude,   five hundered
FUKI,   success   and fifty percent
good cop bad cop
Bad knee.   game leg
Santa Monica
Sylvan Realty
                    FORBIDDEN BROADWAY

DANGER RANGER

This fragrant handkerchief
is heartbreakingly startling.

Ship to Shore, flagrantly lies water.

The idea from last night was,
you're in a room waving
when your arm flies off.

So then you're calm cool and collected
and go call an ambulance.

But now your other arm wants to go too!
Then punches you to death cause you won't let it.

To be said in an oracular tone of voice:
        "The Body
         and
        The Head."

Ten dollars sitting to my left
on the gray shelf.
"Let's rig this light"
is the sort of thing they (the dollars)

like to say

or "'tis the contours"

have you noticed?

are myself.

Myself, the Danger Ranger.

BLAZE, FIRE, SHOCK, CLOVE

What is sculpture?   like bridges?

why bother.

eccentric impulse

shiny metal stuff, DESIGN.

Totem poles are cool.   I'm not mechanically inclined

my hands bleed easily, how can I be hungry

when I just ate all those Pirouettes?

there you have it, the crux.

a car drove over a cardboard carton out in front

A person passed, whistling, morning was here

sun came up.

I've got bergamot, sandalwood and big spaces

those are oils, and a bottle of Joy, world's costliest fragrance

and a tiny bottle of stinky smelling

"magie noire" someplace around here

an empty bottle of diorella which

they stopped making, some white shoulders

body lotion, dwarf size tube.

And a box of fragrant bath cubes

Gardenia, damask rose, Blue Hyacinth.

A. Monteux orange flower water, blue bottle

with creamy yellow label, touches of red, white, olive

Produced in France. french Jasmine

in the bathroom from Kiehl's.

Also, nail polish, Rose Kerala, golden apple, Siesta

Brasier, Little Red Russet, and Oeil de Tigre(!).

some eyeshadows   earth gold steel sage glacier

rouge: Wild Rose, from Clinique

Lipsticks, blaze, fire, shock, clove and the peculiar Antioch Brown.

Also oil of olay, vlemasque, pretty feet & hands

don't buy revlon, anti-apartheid boycott

I don't get sculpture at all

though it is allegedly gratifying on multiple levels.

TROUNCED

Now you're on time.   for once
New   TROUNCED!

& a film.   FSLN Federal Soda
Mercedes Sosa.
Sweaters funded with mercy.

Listen sonny, to those hasty Indians twisting.

What a bitch.
pink fluff or fuzzy ruby

Mr. Shakespeare's diamond pattern

I met a penny in the gutter on Perry Street

You must be crazy, why did I write with CRATONS?

Dinner would be nice,

I would make a little space for myself with a spatula.

SHOPPING SPREE

big heart splattered across the century
immortal bits stuck on the walls of the future

a cutout of a still of Robert Mitchum.

I gleaned hours of unauthorized
inspiration

the sparkling wheel of your smile
ferris wheel circling at night
above an amusement park

all those lights meant to be seen as exaggerated stars

floating in the sky over an industrial valley
with a mall with waterfall or cedarwood
water wheel, goldfishes and pennies

throwing money away for good luck

*

when will this be over?

from now on I intend to be too busy to
ask, even

and go on shopping sprees
spend all the money, get evicted

dirt road
wasted shotgun shells
beyond all the good or bad stuff is where you
find the thoughts you can really strangle and bruise

When I see shoes, socks, clothes around on the street
hanging off fences, so forth
I wonder how they got there.
Kind of scary, don't you?

INADEQUATE QUESTIONS

more craving

red clock,   read the

clock, get up now—

w/ bluebirds,   spatters

what a place,   where there's

Tickertape!   One of the ones

Physical phenomenon

reeling, left me

written in confetti

One Zoo

relaxed   Crawling

Crawling

the physical

into a crawl space

Red snapper, red clicks

an interior monumentally embellished

with camels   "a la fox with spots"

hospital kitchen.

Now they appear to be crazy

people.   crazy

pastiche.

                     people

but what do I care, or

for why do I care?

                             won't you say Dear

                                    Person

                               Person endures

SONG FOR ALICE

Is that you across the road there
in the woods with a flashlight?
Some storm!
Blue spiders of electricity—
I am thinking right now of the clown of the desert.

Beneath a twirling parasol
the image drug succumbs
entirely to itself
implanted in the midst of glut
and bits of trash
a silvery voice
seemingly from under the sea
turning to ashes.

A SENSE OF RUIN

Dignified sheet of cloud, as you pass
in the same gang of images with giants, dinosaurs & ships
great buildings toppling in slow motion,—demolished
how they go by, engaged in the tremendous booming
of their own passage, separate, ignorant
far away.
Why does everything take so long to do, I
can hear your voice in the booming
someone said, "he loved you" to me
and here we are again

*

Fixated on the silhouette of a parking meter
gold and oil moire floating down the gutter
what was, it was.

*

Trixie Timmons will appear dressed today in a bottle green
velvet gown with a train 50 feet long, she's gonna
have a hair-do encumbered with replicas of the nina,
pinta, santa maria.   Tiny shoes of crystal.
since everybody's dressed up all the time these days
you might as well really go all out.
Hand me my pocketbook.

SPARKLING WHITE TOAST

Sparkling white toast ordered by the guy at the next table
lifted my mood.

According to him, every other kind is weird, of course.

I wish while I was watching I wasn't jealous of her.
I kept thinking she's not as good as I am, but because
she *seems* better, everyone'll love her more, I guess
she's the new one now, they'll be really glad to get rid of
me, BACKWARD ACCULTURATION.
I'm going to write an "attitude work."
ASK FOR IT BY NAME.

*

Ask for solutions to your problems in your dreams.
Before you go to bed, ask your dreams to solve your
problems for you.
HOW NICE.

*

You're so sunny & flat and blue
whenever you come in the trees swaying and flashing
outside the window are demoted.

Bandana festooned shopping cart, ONE FOR THE STYLE
BOOK.

Have you noticed what they're wearing?

Here comes Lizzie, ancient collie, which we used to call all of
them Lassie, poor old Lizzie, with a hairless rope for a
TAIL.

HERMIT GIRL OF VENUS

This scenario depicts myself as a flying mermaid
defending a petite lingerie shop from attack
by several unattractive flying mermaids
one of them an evil queen with an ash blonde beehive hair-do.

My life dream of love, l'amour, is to spend one month
in your embrace, intoxicated by the songs you sing
by the stories you tell. That is the dream I dream,
that is my sad impossible dream vision.

What man would be so cruel as to melt this snowy breast?

What god could answer the question that has never been asked.

My sisters drift steering along the Van Allen belt
strumming minuscule platinum harps, crying tears
which do not become raindrops

As a flying mermaid I am required to smash the window
with a chair to hasten pursuit of the reprehensible assailants.

What grief it causes me to do so, for in my home
we cherish the reflective qualities of glass above all else.

Every innocent sparrow who flies credulously into a picture
window is an honored martyr to our cause.

SINGLE FILE

What a nice round face
like a robin

funny.   funny.

Die Valkyrie
the place is full of them

in the beauty of the world
I think I meant to say

I have the career I have always
wanted

it's called

mañana

vines climb the wall one at a time
inch by inch they scale the stucco
a lone rose perfumes the entire "jardin"

enchanted parents slumbering on a marble bench

Chicago Peace

A SPIN OF THE SPHERE

Happy birthday, even though   we aren't in a green room with a

        golden ceiling

your birthday isn't today

but please accept   the blueness of the very sky

my symbolic gesture, an   oracular stunning expendable

        Ship Ahoy! How lucky you are to be in my head

poignant methodology   bruised blossom smelling of lemons   desires

metric fiasco, metro-

nomic maniac metropolis   knotted into a wheeling perchance

and these manacles, not   the way we meant to be

        floating into the grandness of shove

mantra, tubular in all its   facial aspect

exquisite splendour,   items   which create arousal, ardence

arduous journey, my own   paws present indication

trembling offer of amour

        shifts

        the blessing of breath   out of the general

for you to delect, for   missing the day to gain the night

with energy intact

accept peacefully   the gentle aggravation of behavior

my time capsule,   a molecule with

        your name on it, red fading explosively

a genuine   suspect   the sunset abdicates

        to the shy queen of evil, what you gain

stainless steel embroidery   without argument in Venice planted deep beneath   pottery shards, primal remnant

cities' roar and boom   with a spin of the sphere

                             *

even though my inventiveness   stays itself and shamefully

lacks your capability   the "structure"   choosing to be inherent

will be taken as your own   by Those Still Dead

winning extension   and by extension good luck

to you and all your kind!

FORTY YOUS

You and your kitchen
on the phone and doing dishes
I like what everyone likes about you
and its visibility

airplane propeller

offhand, big changes, in your material
the wait in D
sunny railroad platforms, on O platforms
departments, terminals
clanging, whistling, foreign soap

all the way first encounters with modern
return to turn
trace to place
the ambivalence of machinery

machine guns in olive groves

orange groves

mandarins, I guess I'm supposed to be envious

out of control and full of regret

mad that you have a plan for my feelings

When you look at me that way I could slap you

get off, snow falling in the forest on a sunny day

Christmas card, she's walking down a long snow covered
country road at 3 a.m. inside a tv set

a parody of knowing who she is and what she wants
at last.   Dionne Warwick singing

get off   get off   get off

velver.   names, their names are ultimately unimportant
you're lucky to be here, and through no fault of your own
I'm not sorry

a deck of cards, headlines clipped
magazine clipping of a cunt crossed by long red
fake fingernails

we were talking about her hands, how
lovely they were

I'll tell you what to read

killing time.

MORALS IN ABEYANCE

ASPASIA
Criticizes manners.   training of women in Socratic Aeschines.

He was looking at the girl in an embarrassing way
as if though forcing her to uphold his romantic ideal.

I LIKE A BIRDBATH

I ran up to Bruce's
with a postcard
misdelivered
into my hands
"AIX EN PROVENCE"
I read the message
and forgot it
I like a birdbath
I like a birdbath
was what Bruce's
record he was playing
was saying
Susie, go downstairs
and cook your lamb chop
men are so often
wrong about women in
literature!
Simply because
they write with
cardboard boxes
dipped in coffee
Becoming European
is not my goal
I like a birdbath
I like a birdbath

HEMMING AND HAWING, BOWING AND SCRAPING

I did what I did because I had to talk to you

Magic Dial

my pill, one hour ago

strangler ex-cops the tuffest meanest

a low blow

poor scott   nervewracking

polka dot curtain

deep sea diving off the waters of

Kona   a silent unreal quality

Whirlybirds on the parker ranch

fearless Mt. Goats

In a world ever changing

it is comforting to know

men with sticks

centered in justice

the whistle

dumb jerks

hit this place tomorrow night

ethics officer

FROM THE TWELFTH FLOOR OF 170 FIFTH AVENUE

to the north the sky is yellow and it's snowing

right across the way a woman in a pink shirt was shaking

a dust rag from a window of the historic Flatiron Building.

THE THING STICKING IN MY MIND IS THE SUNSHINE

Next door so to speak the con ed plant

is making a tremendous racket, like a broken car two stories

long, now things are popping away out there radiator style

scraping leaves, grapevines or similar, breezing

on down the street, a cab door slams, Cinnie disembarks

If and when I make a movie it will be of Sister Edna Perry

or you, standing on the McGraw-Hill building observation deck

staring down at the world below, where 4 a.m. is absent

because we got older?   I mean to say,

what we can look forward to?

with the wind blowing our pretty hair about our ears

YYYYYYYYYYYYYYYYYY

is pale.

LITTLE LIFE, BELGRADE

Four new records, 20 voices

the lush particulars of a moose herd on 14th st.

antiquarian or a snap to

black and white photo of traffic, noonday

Belgrade, November 19, 1963.

Frank O'Hara, Adventures In Poetry

in the half light, wait in the parlor, incense

threadbare oriental rugs

maroon, the prince of Moscow

wear a fez, the bathrooms of the twenties

he died in Palermo, creeping toward the divider

girls from ballet school

the boy looked at Johnny, Tim

milk's.   When I look at this box what do I really see?

Severini's cheerful choo choo train pulling into where

Kneipp?   Paris.   with orange sun and disjointed landscape

kilometers, a storm rising as they save their

circular hats, into the far distance the hats roam

workmen at the corn palace

your willing face, Steve's "so dear"

Oh the tinfoil on cigarettes, elusive, how daily items

will become artifacts in several years

to grant their past has a future

and they'll be with you then

then were will be then

LOCKED FROM THE OUTSIDE

Japanese beetles plague, pester peonies, when unnecessary

how clear, maybe they paint the bottle white so they can

give you less, maybe

Jasmin hurled from a window by her dusted uncle

lives vary tremendously   shell pattern, fish fountain

                              on church

in collaboration with the present   Madonna, good at heart

minute, 90 degrees   dear   inept void where heart should be

                    mistaken for kindness

beads of rain on a maroon car   moral rant, statement

                                    sentiment, settlement

the car seemed to be bleeding!   all news antique

except for Senator Byrd whose suave parliamentary gesture

through the mist in a crowded auditorium, blocked a crooked

pass, gaping, pretending to witness what failed to even pose as event

a nude female leads two goats   appointment

without breathing the slightest filigree of breath

through a ferny mountain pass in the twilight

burning, burnt, should have, will, you he it, the we I

can't go wrong with basics though to do so would be refreshing

the present minute is discouragement   twinkling strobes

tenses,

here is where you cause something to happen   I mean you have a body

liable to the subjunctive

to do

         MAGIC.   namely

as opposed

urgently desiring transcendence, as called

Friday signifies oppression, by which calling, had called

WAR

meaning   You tried to leave but the door was locked.

war

locked from the outside.

What an insult.   What is an insult, or what is "cute".

War.

Not doing homework

War, the ultimate in neoclassical junk

being subjected

now go back and install beauty, restore virtue

I had a painter in mind   arid

guys   tv in a doorway on first avenue

angular, demonic, tormented by evil.

for the sake of the pastoral two notes

trees are giant plants surrounding us

how can we live

before vanishing

Mary McCarthy wrote Edith Wharton wrote gardens of Italy

are arranged as if each part were a room.

AVENGER, AVENGING SPECTRE PAUSES, CONTEMPLATES, GROWS CALM

consider

joyous abandon approached in increments

yellow fields, french impressionist

appointment calendar, horse and cart

crossing bridge

one goes toward the source of unhappiness

to scrutinize, instead of fleeing with dread as before

in nightmares, run over by truck

dread overwhelming

TOUR THE PERPENDICULAR

Brown recluse, Brown spinster

three is a great time for swinging large
bags back and forth with a friend

an upsurge in years
releases the cast of utility

NO PIGMENT

City of Beautiful Towers
is what they call
COPENHAGEN

      THE THORN ROOMS

are on my mind today,
   on my side today,   in

damask, and yet the
        song of the Marchelin, warbling
requires the
stomping bloody feet of soldiers

nicer person, meaner
art.   N.Y.

                no matter how
snide
they seem always
to be polite and   neatly
9:15 to 5:15

dressed

dry sand.   spare weather

space under construction

I was happy til I saw I'd have no windows

in my new office

On the walls of my new office, no windows.

DRAWN TO GARBAGE, DRAWN TO FLAME

Fragment structured according to a set of criteria

FURNISHED

by a blemished psyche

pleasant conversation with self upon waking.

get all dressed up to hunt for guy

think I'm going out of my way

think I don't care

think my legs look big and fat

even in black stockings

think I don't care

A GHOSTLY SHARK

A ghostly shark
three pianos wide
or long, Ann says the water is sex
but maybe Ann is sex instead!
attached to the back of the downtrodden
an inadvertent sign saying
FUCK KABIR
oh me, oh my

giant baskets filled with every fruit
are purported to be a great luxury
but I don't care for fruit so much
I like chocolate

all I ever wanted the only thing I ever wanted
the one thing I ever wanted out of life
was to be King of the People.

Burn incense to be like you.
wear Tyrian Purple.   retire early
all I ever wanted the only thing I ever wanted
the one thing I wanted out of life
was to feel you up.

and burn you up, baby, if I may be so bold

detergent.

THE INSISTENCE OF MORE LURE

If only I were *her*,

in an elegant black wool dress

simple solid jewelry

the person who knows precisely what to do

perched on a darling gilt throne

forehead clear, happy in a

complex sort of way

handsome adult men who wear suits

hanging around

no cash transactions

all my clothes delivered

wrapped with tissue paper

in boxes striped pink and black

I get so mad at this abuse

the insistence of being more lure,

alluring

but there where I've been

the moon is shining

plashing fountains

leafy copse

and many wrong things happening

a troupe of seventeen year old

Iron Maiden freaks puking inside their tent

chopping up the orchard lawn with

Dad's Oldsmobile

and what about these crass mosquitoes?

GOOD ENERGY IS COMING

shadows resting at the foot of the east

a new invisible

the right side

of a guy stepping past some honeysuckle bushes

in a courtyard

family is all

especially in pieces

ornate railing of empire

Northern California

Mass and Marble

Ivy and dead air

Good energy is coming

to me through the

table.   Let's

go camping

swimming and fishing

who cares if I can

read or write

let's.

*

Dear Mr. Scientist, if you're so smart, how come you make
all this junk that doesn't work. How come you don't know
the difference between going backward and quitting while
you're ahead. If you're so smart how come you're only
doing your job.

IN THE KIND OF WORLD WHERE WE BELONG

You've got a hole in your head and you
stuff it with money
yesterday I had a collision
and told him laughingly
I'd been planning for a long time
then I said
in the kind of world where we belong
you've got a hole in your head
and you stuff it with money
New York Senate Okays Death Penalty
aid approved to El Salvador
be more specific

Who are the real killers.
P I G S written on the pavement down there
2 women next to me talking about
"Ill Days"
wage slaves
her fat wrist pinched by a watch
and underneath the watch
is a runny sore, she's
allergic
"PIGS"

every day is an "Ill Day."

UGLY FACADE

Wood dipped in plastic
wood coated with plastic
somewhere uptown is an ugly facade
next door to where a friend of mine
who's a painter had a job

the people with the ugly facade, and we
don't have to mention who they were, though
you would definitely know who I was talking about

then I'm moving, my mind downtown and to the west
where optically pure sailboats emerge and dissolve
on an austere line, glaucous rolls of water
bounce to and fro at the five o'clock position
as if we were at six, a bird with a body but no head
some rich people in a yacht named Sunny Queen
heading north upriver where we were
before the conversation about wood dipped in plastic.

This bird has a crook for a neck, and these rich
people with their intimidating boats are
stirring up wake in our drinking water.

SMALL BLACK BEETLES

They are only small black beetles

nothing to be afraid of

the forests of Finland.
level gazing at woodpeckers outside Helsinki airport

same weather as yesterday, Memorial Day

fear not, he Sails above the stormy weather

can't you hear a miniature voice rising up?

we saw:

the Towhee
the Floridian Gallinule
the Oystercatcher
the Green Heron
some of us,
the Glossy Ibis
Purple Finches
Goldfinches
Tree Swallows
Brants, Canadian Geese
Snowy Egret
the Ruddy Turnstone
the Killdeer
the Ringed Plover
Ruddy Ducks

in flight from ticks
I jettisoned my Kelly green cheap umbrella

remember when we were standing in the downpour on Third
Avenue and Thirteenth Street

watching the clock?

I hate that song, a girl said just now in front of me,
The number one.

FAT PEN

The penis mightier than the sword.
What has been taken away,
filmy snap of a small girl

            Being yelled at

"Take It!".

I miss you
on my left

            You might
             enjoy this
       "I decided I'd be there"
            But

in last night's episode
we took a drug
shaped like
multi-colored
wagon wheels
in a goldfish
food holder
on the bus.
            If I'm hurting

you please let me know

Now when I said those words, I woke up

the nicest minute

was when I leaned

over and put

my arm on you.

THREE ROLLS

Three rolls of film
yellow black and white
resting by the periwinkle penny vase on my desk
to be taken and developed on
avenue of the americas

monumental high rise construction
is endemic
the clock on con ed is no longer visible, due
to hideous zeckendorf plaza towers, not from west
leastwise.

sleep peacefully drunk
dream my baby turns into a weasel, bites my tit
with sharp little needle teeth
have another cookie.
day two

There's a station wagon outside, looking like a shoe.
a girl appeared on the scene with two matching dogs
I had a negative response, stylish but felt
bad for the dogs being a display for this girl's
personality, envious I guess, should feel sorry for all;
do—feel sorry for christmas trees.
Hacked Down In Their Prime.

a friend, her mom sent her a can of anchovies

for christmas, Hi Jane. Seasons Greetings

No more faith in my writing, no more bursting with excitement

fairly sad tonight, no lovers, boyfriends, city

is shithead mean, outsider is me.

GRECIAN FORMULA

every drop falling drop
is landing on a designated spot
implied religious doctrine
who's watching, who knows.

Boss Romaine

scraps of lettuce in wet cartons heaped tragically on the sidewalk

you're staring at a small point
between my eyes, or the bulletin board
in a mere routine to evoke intense emotion
steadfast desire.

an iron eagle rose and spread its wings then
crumpled, convulsed.

Muscles falling all around in great clumps
of lavender delight, the Spanish soul torn asunder

a mouth that has forgotten the difference
between kissing and eating

love slave in tube sox.

BOULEVARDS FOR GHOSTS

When stars do shine with points above
I will find some marble stairs
Where I may safely undertake
To lay my weary burden down

You standing there, you standing there
10 a.m. sunlight on the Meadowlands Arena

You standing there, you standing there
Held together by bits of clothesline

You standing there, you standing there
Buildings rise like ladders from the heart of Manhattan

When the sun was coming up
What we saw through the windshield was
Another stormy morning dawning
Purple clouds towering above the plain

It never fails to blow my mind
I've seen that face a thousand times
In the movies or on the checkout line
I've seen that face a thousand times

Bedizened with shattered containers
Evidence of beverages consumed by a fire burning within
The avenues in our locale glitter so fabulously
They have boulevards for ghosts

I'm going to stand at the bus stop now
I'm going to launch all my worries
Into the pale blue atmosphere
Today, where sexy clouds again will treat them to oblivion;

To drift or snap, a taffeta ribbon
Affixed to an air raid siren
Is no relief.

VALENTINE'S DAY 1985

MR. HOLLY

Mr. Holly sprang up
and gazed at the stars.

You are my friend
for a million years.
for a million years.
for a million years.

Water running from a cooler
into a paper cup

BABY WITH A GUN

what to do—why don't you tell me

your methods are always better

than mine, kind of like a

baby with a gun

stepped over shadows

christmas tree burning

<u>WILD</u>

can't manage

it break it

let it happen

wind up to

want to give up

be a sculptor

have nice house

blue light bulb

go home, read, be smart

go ahead, open the refrigerator

this here is <u>HOME</u>

experience description

examine the urge to describe

feelings

description is impossible

description altruistic

altruism nonexistent

state of mind

How

can you provoke curiosity

it's all what you heard!

How can I make this place?

A FORM OF PRAISE

The empty wrapper of an angel is asking me
if I'm ready

Go to your window
now take a piece of the sun pie.

BAMBOO UNION

One day is the same as another to me

at six o'clock young beauties with blank resistant expressions
and matching shoes cut down into the dark
while above us to the west
light falls on the movie industry
mountains, plains, farms, hills, then us
in reverse order, you carry your mishaps
wherever you go, to the grave
as if though the past were a wreck in a borrowed
car fifteen years ago

I know you hate me, but too bad, if you hate me

Amazing audience tells you what's been banned
my pussy, that's what, ostrich feathers

no sweat

mayhem   off the wall   who I've admired most

grudging admiration   fuel.

PAY ATTENTION

cerise suede   guide   I furniture the place

nesting lodges pine needles   dizzily encouraged

exercise   bubble bath   retiled lined with lizard

and a huge scarlet bow

                          waking seriously

redefined   all wrong   an ok leaving a third bit

avocet   out or invisible triangle

          why must one pay attention?   nothing doing.

           pretend I'm you beneath a sheet of Water drownded

Pay

necklace

when you happened upon us we were deprived of incident

we hate idiotic things way they are

ample roving, another word, blame for sight, VISIBILITY

quaking lamp

hand me, PAY ME

calls

to the right, a net for snag of heart

sun   over   rocks

lighter fluid

swings back double to snag

intimately brilliant suggestive portraits

THE NEW
OLD PAINT

2010

ON THE DAILY MONUMENT

I WILL TELL

I will tell of my aspirations
philosophy of self-improvement
transitory metaphor
continuous thought

contrasting grand
with down to earth

social settings
embarrassing situations
humble tombstones

an unusual acquaintance

a prayer to the authorities

a plea.

a narrative or tale in sense only

a bird detached from the huge heap
of information over on the side.
flies up.   grackle.   sits on branch with
leaves, sings.   Rocks.

WHO WILL WASH THE GARBAGE

Remember when they grafted genes from the fireflies
onto tobacco plants?

Can dogs smell spiders?

Is rust contagious?

Who will wash the garbage?

To me, a landscape is like a very beautiful woman.
I paint trees with their leaves up.

origami display at the U.N. c. 1967

earrings, earrings from Thailand
you make me happy, my only real jewelry
you've heard every dumb thing I said
earrings
with tiny pyramids of droplets

once again pearls drop onto the opera
the great club of winter
downtown buildings rise as if from amherst

clouds stretching southwest over the church

screaming kids evacuate 12th street school at 3 p.m.

Fussy siblings holding hands three stories down

Silver jet high high way off in the air

Endless leisure.

FROM THE SILVER PAVILION

green skyscrapers on eve of St. Patrick's day
emerald city

postcards of flowers from Susan, map of Caribbean from
Peggy,
headache keeps me slow
running   walking   standing still
the eternal triumvirate
I have an ailment!   so boring
crumpled kleenexes, accumulated clutter

smooth down, straighten up, carry on, windmills, mill
wheels

clownish tulips from Sue
bow their heads

you are nut
you are craz
don't be sill

an excess of nouns in need of hobby activity
I feel a wrenching in my legs, yes.

GROANING PIGEONS

something to be designated later occurs in the flu minute.

she saw the baby, she was pissed, sent snakes.
They went to eat the baby eagerly, but the baby
gripped and strangled the horrid beings.

he stood dumbfounded in wonder
hard to endure but delightful.   PINDAR,   NEMEAN I

I waited for you like a fiend in the sunlight.

tigers enjoy swimming. in socorro n.m., thunderstorms
everyday of July and August

Greg gives me $100.   and we all fall asleep on cafeteria
tables.
caught in blue carpeted well where I cannot breathe or
call out

they seem to be sociable (waving flipper)

                    but really are quite shy
                              (cover face with flipper)

COO COO VISION

I could see myself standing there
with a flip hair-do and a poorboy
my feet shod in thick shoes

a wild assortment of humble things—
nuts and bolts, forks, tea bags, keys, whistles,
thankful one dimensional daisies—
approached from across the railroad tracks

every noun was there,
in close, present, Chartreuse . . . Tangerine.
They were close to myself, contained.

There also was movement, then as now, movement out.

*

Dryness, kindness, flowers
interacted freely with lush English sounds

Suddenly an overwhelming fragrance of lilacs
came gushing
through our car window
Hush!   the god of love is nigh

to magnify my internal décor

dusty chintz curtains, spots of sun, view of the playground

You were a distorted rationale crumbling into a line:

I Forgot.

*

After a length of time I came to imagine I understood
this vision
Chartreuse and Tangerine

the coo coo colors of Donna

TINY TEARS

Tiny Tears, I loved you
so much I cut off your
fingers and toes
with my safety scissors

*

I loved to rock you to sleep
and watch your lashy eyelids
close in measured increments

click click click

*

Later on, I thought it was
funny to put your head
on Barbie's body.

I'm sorry, and I'm really sorry

about that time I left you out in the backyard

all night,

Tiny Tears.

THE SULLEN SHEPHERDESS

Sullen shepherdess propped
against a stump
a web is connecting your uplifted skirt to the stump
and you are broken
here in the country

                          *

You are a spiderweb hanging from a lamp
hello, spider, spiders OK, mosquitoes OUT.
next to a honey jar filled with wildflowers
Bouncing Bet
you are nature, somehow kind
Patricia is nice, I like her boys
Gabriel and Michael
everyone is nice but not me
yes you are, you're nice too, you're
everyone

                          *

I'm your voice. Didn't you know? I'm not really
ashamed to say so, it's almost a job, nature
and your ceaseless voice, ceaseless pine forest whoosh
abovehead, an owl hooting with melancholic enthusiasm
Jack Benny on Route 66
high wide and lonesome
will not be denied
lunar eclipse
world voices comprehend
I'm thinking about sex, ichneumon
wasp can't leave that broken lamp alone
flashlight navigators

what are their reasons?   broken sexy radio, worthless to begin
with,   stars all over the sky.   our field is great!   fresh
we can't stop chirping
or splashing

HORRIBLE VALENTINE

flap flop flap flop   inside   my head

poignant foam rubber bells

of true love

*

true love
made of candy lipstick
and vaseline

smeared on the wall

dirty mayonnaise jar
filled with brown water

and blood splattered on the wall

*

"Through the wilderness," said my mother
"run through the wilderness quickly darling and seek help."
there was not time to lose

RUSSIAN FOLK SONGS

I have no mother,
I have no father,
I was born from the street
I was born from a chicken egg

*

As we float on a stinking lake
I kiss your slimy lips
and you hold me close to your hairy chest

*

Mary, Mary, your legs are so white and lovely
let us watch while you wash them in the river—
Be quiet, you noisy geese! My mother-in-law
is asleep beneath that bush.

A SNOWFLAKE AND A BALL OF YARN

I heard the sound of the mitts
here from California to see you

stay cotton

the first knot is the
who was gone and touched noses

*

trying he went southerly
standing in the shower to see fall

one of these things is awful!

*

I get down so I won't recognize
the show

I won't be finite.
Oh summer is dead

If I get it in Manhattan
the sky looks like

he won't even—
Hold on!

HEXAGONS IN THE HALLWAY

I mean why
take the heat
this is just my house
when early cold
bounces loudly
through the form

*

see why its

    OK

O home

    *

The hundred husbands
something's standing watch over
me

so
  far out!
Federal Lands

you're so brushy

RHAPSODY IN ORANGE

I don't know why I love you!
    HI!

white tight accept.   God
what is.   So.

    *

The wife is so slow like a
stupid sunboat.

If my legs aren't long is no
see how long.   a crowd.

    *

These bottles are the most!

Might is the Phaser.

THE TURNPIKE BOMBER

we were talking beneath the
moon going over the house
on a sofa in the garden on
the phone.

*

SHOW ME THOSE COVETED HORSES
Show   me   those   coveted   horses

come to the future party & do
kayaking with a gun with me

*

oh how it's so old, the same singing
lantern. maybe tonight someone will marry you.

young boy see how

what to do the light takes
them and trades them
hides them

INTO THE STICKERS

the chairs appear to be walking up the lawn from the beach

what I'm noticing today isn't pointed swelling or reproductive

equipment failure isn't my fault, consolation

bald spot on grass making a   C

must I converse?

exploit your circumstances, nothing else

I want to let them sit there so I can watch them

quietness

two owls up in a dead white tree

beach blanket falling into the stickers

graveyard by the caribbean, washing into the sea

decomposing creatures in a stricken village

NO WONDER

I wish I could provide myself with more allowance and the
wide open

sand

                            snow

plastic hearts

coral twigs washing up

               *

rain attacking the huge noisy window
sitting on a friend's radiator

               *

wring out bathing suit.
moon so bright I can see the other part

in a small town it's horrible, you feel trapped.

THE OTHER SIDE OF TOWN

I refuse to depart from my companion

the radar will be out for another ten hours

many small electronic parts, transistors resistors
Easter basket

furious rapping at the shutter becomes
tornado

there was always more surface on the other side of town

How heavenly to clear the overgrowing weeds
to enter and say in a voice clear and loud
I Want.

Maybe when he hears I came looking for him he'll call me
but he heard I like him, and he didn't call.

I hate and despise your ridiculous ex, I'm
never going to defer to the needs of a stranger again.
Shame shame shame on me.

FULCRUM OF DISASTER

leaning against the gate on st. marks place I realized its from
the viewpoint of the sky
the yonder
storm sign with elevation omitted

good kissing or making out is the same as condensed rockabilly
drummer ghost or a hypnotized wolf with two x's for eyes swallowing
shifting.
[initial flaw]

distance is the same as time, emptiness is a kind of speed moving
slowly with extreme consciousness.   the distance
belongs to somebody else, secondary concern was dictated
to the weaver, intact but invisible

I felt like a piece of lace made from ice
or I felt like three blue stars
streetlight in the yellow leaves of a ginkgo tree, I felt the cold
dark iron of the fence, I felt compressed, energized, sparkling.
[but I was mistaken, and so we arrive at the fulcrum of disaster]

one week ago
enormous conglomerate snowflakes

tumbled and careened down the brick wall

whirling around in bare branches

embraced by dead grapevines

[I wish you didn't love me so much]

[I never had a choice]

futile rejoinder

snow is so interior, preoccupied, oblivious, more interior than

my own internal self, I mean it never can snow inside us

inside me I thought about what you might be doing, you're in

my heart now [shrivel] no question, frost beads along my hair

sliding, half skating past the silent abandon in Tompkins Sq. Park.

POEM

Days are short
windows are cold
thoughts of love
go round and round
in my head

they say
the man is a bee,
the woman a flower
but I think you and me
are like a train station in the sun

REBEL STRONGHOLD

First you spurn me as a woman
Claiming you want only to be friends
Then when I attempt to comply
You laugh in my face

grey eminence, ambit, smalt, zaffer, woad
pavonian, verdet,

typical run

the first time I ever sucked someone's dick, machine gun was on the stereo and in my mind's
eye I could see a person shaking Jimi Hendrix by the shoulders with an attitude of mock an-
noyance while he was singing the words machine gun so that's how I made it for Tom Merkle

checkered flag at the starting line

here on thursday nite   a crummy ache behind my eyes
push, squeeze, spin
transformed!
into an orchid

instead I come out friday morning—"a martini in my throat"

ON THE DAILY MONUMENT

Lookouts posted on either end of the street
my sole objective is to
visit you before you change your address

I used to want to be closer, now I want to be
closer too, as in "closerness"

deliver new framework, dispense
with retrograde behaviors
hush
sigh
how curly hair is organized innocence
grandma's persian lamb
cloud sails out over sea, independent
ship afloat on   mirror of   enough

enough.
                 enough

on out over sea

*

                 hen exit
               please do   ass
               in front of us

sound nature, leaden authenticity haunts fragments
shattered neon, one a.m.
frail plea for the daily monument
crunching underfoot

quiet room, I want to be clear

also

resemble soda pop, shoot

cherrie pits at taxi cabs

east river enters my head through my nose

    looking into your eyes I feel like a voyeur

the happy taste of an orange explodes in my mouth

*

sign on wall,   infantilism

when I hear healing mentioned I think of band-aid smell
& poisonous green disinfectant soap

be still, retreat. so you can turn misery into hair ornaments
or wipe catfood bits from off counter

ESTIMATION

Sun shines through the stockade

into our billowing then   (tent)   Greg and Jennie's

underneath crashing breakers' swirl

helpless seaweed masses, band-aids

there's a black dog up on the dune hill

with a total stranger

surveying the beach at Ditch Plains

I can't pick you out below

satisfied, relieved, to be secret again

beach roses proliferate, honeysuckle proliferates

the revenues

of love

deteriorate

optically

COMMITTEE ON DARKNESS

sexually repellent

hammering, car going thru

fire hydrant fountain, woman

calling Jose

sun on my back, Monday

I must be fair

historically accurate

but I ache .

from left to right

negative universe

being told.

disconnected from the

cypher

YOU LOSE

My love is qualified as a rising complaint

—   out the window

downtown, august windows across Walker street

north side only,
sun's intensity bleaching sediment,   limestone

arches, Poe or Nevada

blank eyes

bonding honking, freight elevator bells
and unidentified clacking

chance concentrated in a ring

RITUAL ASPECT

gravity

tension in the

rhyming of weather

change

*

swaying trees

palsied airplane

cheerful errand, traffic

directions to friends

house

TWEETING birds

unhappy landlord

people with new baby

May

neighbor running water

more coffee

forgotten toothbrush

dusty blankets

yard sale

*

headlights from toyota on foggy beach over a rise

in the dunes, corona of light shining mysteriously

at the bottom of a semi-circle waves appear

ghosts walking off a ledge into the nether world again & again

STOP DROP ROLL

The ten plagues:

Hail

Locusts

Darkness

Beasts

Cattle-plague

Boils

Blood

Frogs

Lice

First-born

*

concertina wire

you remind me

of my shopping cart

How am I going to

move when fall arrives

Chirping sparrows

Hummingbirds in the chollas

Sphinx moths.

The desert is

Full of germans with cameras

They're way out west

*

You were telling me
My new short hair
Needs to be washed
More often

*

This amazing project is guaranteed to
Generate its own resources—
And they will proliferate exponentially

RABBITS BROKE THE WALL

a gorgeous knot of words hovers before my face
when I fall asleep

aphids swarming on a bunch of dead chrysanthemums
sag harbor kitchen sink

the jargon of pealing bells
propels my line into the star guide

*

I cry my eyes out

I would do absolutely anything.

I guess I would

*

twilight

       hedges

        the highway

birds fly over

CHICKADEES
IN THE SNOW

GONE NOW

David stepped into the falling snow falling in the parking lot.
cells—whatever guaranteed those billowing sails
in your head,
It's gone now

FROM THE MIDDLE OF THE ROAD

not enough cleavage, dude

save me,

save you from me

something like that

seriously, a person is crossing the

street. If you laugh a lot

you won't be taken seriously and

you're right!

Now the clouds bend down over this

unhappy valley

I like tits, but only my own,

first nasty

street slander, thought of 1000 snappy

rejoinders and then went on my

way to the church bazaar

like Jesus.

Those clouds hound the valley, go away!

Let the illuminated shrubs in the

park alone. Let me buy some gold foil

garlands

not ponder evil

I've never been to any of the rocks I see

up there, don't know how to get up there,

smell of frankincense where?

insert Grand Central

now we're back here, it happens again

a person crosses the street. Another one

crosses the opposite way, young guy a punk, waiting for the

bus. Pretty dress

black and fuchsia voile. I check my credit card

like a grown up debtor, decide to

spare myself the humiliation of its being no

good. The wallet I bought on impulse

is no good, burgundy

leather, might as well belong to Aunt Claire—

elegant gold snap. There's probably

a particular name for that clasp,

within the industry. I like

to look at goods in store windows

and imagine the moment of fabrication

guess how many steps were required

I want to speak French

don't want to study it

hurts my teeth, to be so ignorant

of all the rooms in this

magnificent palace.

Ice skating. You should

know how! You might need to use

that skill to get away, make your getaway

Hans Brinker and the golden skates that's

how I thought Massachusetts would be in winter

Eileen, I dreamt of you recently

but I can't remember where or how

where are those little green grasses

pushing up from melting snow Tues.

ice, Thursday, snow, double whammy

Thanksgiving, Pearl Harbor

TIME IS THE QUEEN OF WEATHER

crossing over a bridge,

      pathetically optimistic world but I feel inspired to like it here
and there may be a baffle, a sweet sort of feeling flips down over and over.

    nothing to go wrong

lacy glass diatoms, a grateful
community dynamic
    dextrally coiled forms

amaze the imagination as they chew tunnels thru the substrate drift along
on rafts of algae. no loss or sorrow only constant

            innovation, and deposition
fill the page, I want to keep talking and talking and singing, about my velvet skirt, there
were clouds earlier tonight, they disappeared

upwelling
snow and stars

no absence

    no weird body count

   no

                    rooms to modify   siphonate in description
void spiral the basis for

                         water falling over me,

                                   unfolding

                                                  wind
down you go
now.
        It's a shade I saw once, in a piano

next morning the sad pulse
of sun coming in,

fading the furniture, making it tired,
        told me
Time is the queen of weather.

DEAD ROAD

if the night were a train
or the highway were a storm

I'd be a cloud
I'd be a cry, I'd come to you as a cloud

you'd sleep
tired tired tired of all images

deep beneath your heart

the noise of a sunny day long ago will hit you
the noise will hit you

and something behind you will fall to
dreaming

going past a cemetery in Hadley
dead of night, dead of winter

headlights only, snowing
heavily, whirling turbulent snow-filled

beams of light
right parallel

to route 9,

I was a dead person dreaming

On a dead road

CHICKADEES IN THE SNOW

Wake up one morning in Massachusetts.
When I woke up

Morning, you're after a snowstorm.
It was the morning after

Sky you are bright blue.
The sky was bright and blue and sunny

Sunshine, make the world sparkle and glisten.
The sunshine made the world sparkle

Snow, fall down.
Big clods of snow fell from pine boughs in the yard,
like fainting ladies
obscuring my splendid view of the airport beyond the fleshy pink
tudor home that sits across the street from number 88.

Fly up,
A crow flew up
into the southernmost Norway Spruce hauling a bagel.

Perfect squirrel tracks in the fresh snow, looping from tree to tree.

Chickadees were buzzing and goofing around.

Snowplow, pass.
Snowplows went by, people were out, scraping off their cars.

In general, this morning
had a festive aura. I have to say I love the changed world
and the cold floors of this
morning morning morning

where you have to shovel if you want to move.

Go to school Anne Marie, make a new start.
Downstairs directly below my three Palladian windows,
the front door slammed and I saw Anne Marie
head down the street on her way to school.

SWEEPING HER SIDEWALK

You have to stop and feel down to your socks

But nothing's there, just a heavy scraping
From distant in the building
Ceasing.

Why do I always end up in the pines?
Now a dog is barking and cars go by
the electronics are real

But, beneath those trees I was safe from insomnia
Confusing myself with Heidi. Wanting a little hayloft
all my own.

LOST VERSES

In my dreams last night
you were singing "waterloo
sunset" but the words were
different. You explained that
you were singing the suppressed
verses, verses which had disappeared
with the advent of assembly line production
and the production of replaceable small metal parts.
"In an assembly line world, individuals are conscripted to aid machinery in completion of a task."
"I believe this song is a celebration of the secret romance people have with their alienation."

FUN IN CINCINNATI

Late on the night of April 15th
when I drove down to the post office to file my taxes
the traffic was all backed up for blocks

hundreds of volunteers were lining the street handing out free donuts,
dressed like clowns, etc. There was music too.

so I found myself creeping toward the post office in a tax time processional eating a donut

a postal employee runs up to your car window, says see you next year!, grabs your envelope runs
a few yards ahead, hands it off to another postal employee
who tosses it away in a white canvas
bin
and it was quite fun

ATTENTION

I can't decide
I won't decide

until I do, and no one can make me.

massive redbuds.

Rising turning,

binding, incising.

acceleration, impact, subtraction.

This works nicely. You don't need to do anything

with it or to it, its just there, in the manner of

pink astroturf or a fork in an eyebrow, or fruit on a table in
Germany

or apple blossoms filling a tunnel

dear memory

please let me never forget the way the air feels today
I'm in the corridor so to speak.

Newark swinging on a hinge, reveals
by the roadside brachiopod shell bed
all imbricated

do you want me to carry you back and forth?

SICK OF PENNSYLVANIA

Pennsylvania, the state of
Not calling, not writing.

Behind every piney mountain a coal mine

Don't go down that road, it'll make you cry

Truly this is God's country,
But only on one side.

I've went to Jersey Shore, and it wasn't what I thought it would be.

The enforced state of letting go

—the aggravating complexities of this irritating Pennsylvania world,

our life,

seem most like.

ARSON

I moved from my old neighborhood to Wrigleyville. Nothing

very good ever happened to me down there. Now I'm living on the corner of Bosworth

and

Waveland where I hope my life will improve. My first night, last night, there was a

terrible

fire just around the corner on Ashland Avenue. A business.

a wooden frame house with an adjacent brick garage

Korean body shop

I couldn't sleep. I took a bath

I went back to bed, but soon there were sirens

sirens screaming

and not going away, and then the campfire smell

Got up, put on some clothes

went downstairs

I came around the corner

there were at least 20 fire engines

and Ashland blocked off.

Billows of dense black smoke piled out of the building. The building

was crackling as it burned. frantic. urgent.

The tar tiles on the side of the building

were melting buckling oozing

High up, two firemen sat astride the beam of the steeply pitched roof

As though riding a great burning horse, using their axes as whips.

chopping holes in the slopes of the roof. They would inch forward and chop another hole.
and flames flickered escaping outward.

I kept going closer and closer until I could feel the heat from the fire warming my face
one of the firemen told me to move back, and I said
it's an instinct, I just feel drawn to it. He said, I know.
but you have to move back, you could get hurt
but the fire was so warm and alive, a hot crazy animal.

A man from the busy bee boarding company made a pass.
Then a guy with a CFD
baseball cap and a bag of raisins passed and asked me, "enjoying the barbecue?"

A fire can be quite a scene.

A coil of heavy smoke was winding and sinking over my building.
This morning large crispy curls of charred tarpaper covered my new street all up and
down the block.

I wonder about the body shop owners, if they were insured, how they got

the dough and experience to start such a business. Where will they go, what will they do?

I went walking by

this morning. first checked the alley,

apple tree in blossom with black charcoal trunk.

gutted.

spoke with a man, the owner of the building

He said it was arson. I asked who was suspected and he said the upstairs

tenants, some "hillbillies".

I asked because, after I took that bath last night, I

stared down out the window onto my new corner. A couple

of tough looking guys pulled up in an old Pontiac, parked in front of my car. They took a

bunch of big square cans from

the back seat. All the while, both looking around furtively.

Then one of

the guys looked up, and they both stared at me watching them, from the third floor

wrapped in my

geranium-red bath towel.

THE RUINED CHAPEL

Remember how in August
you turned your eyes
into the cooling lake
August, but November's
on the way
the lake will be
getting cold, really cold
the woods will simplify
like your face
when leaves will fall
tumble down
to make an orange cover
for the oval planet earth
where we could lie down,
I can see your neck
your plaid shirt, cause
then the stars are so
easy to see, no more
leaves up, interfering
in the signals
they've fallen down
rationally, perfectly
in ovals like your face
in circles
where they've fallen
weepy tears have fallen
into black velvet pools
nets, aching hollows
onto American ridges
simple shale ledges
once an ocean
same as I was
living in the house
of my mom and dad

remember the ravine?
remember the ruined chapel?
remember the stars
of January 1970
plummeting into my
consciousness
down through
slumbering dogwoods
while the sum of
coolness convened in
the woods. Where are you
now? Does this
question commit
me to the arms of the
academy. my heart
opening up stays locked open
what you are
is what I want
for myself and don't
have. Your hips, leaves
in the woods
sun slipping behind
the mountain,
oh, your form.
is what the lake is a memory of
your hair getting gold
as it straggles down
the back of your neck
your neck, your throat
your consideration
your soft gold is so strong
you look kind of hurt
but you're not telling
your oval face is like time
an oval
you whirl your silver square
the lake freezes

your attitude walk
there's the drive
seven lakes drive
the life force
in your car by the lake
getting cold, you
keep on going
keep going
your good natured
golden hair, you
turn your eyes into
a small intensely hungry
effort, impartial
burning.
complicity emerged
a fair medieval oval
your height filled the air around you
with the middle of the world, between high
and low, you were curious, washed by a pale
snow, by a galvanized pail
in a nation narrow as a bridge
nervewracked by the dent between
your stomach and your hipbone
hitchhikers with signs
Russian River, Eureka, DC, New England
brown hills, forlorn landscaping
before the day when I got so alone
without you
when everything was still moving along
optimistically toward a
bright resolution
we convened in the woods
in a plaid
shirt, beneath the easy stars

& like a wheel I cannot bend
like a wheel I cannot bend

WHITE BANDS

watch it, Daisy, I'm ready to race

my front is hollow,

my top is short

from behind I'm succinct

yearn and regret it

my vision is crystal

move the gravel, move it in

now the landscape streaming fades and cools

a million thousand

between two white bands

you have to let go, you want to let go

THE FREAKY WAYS

Row, wicked sailor row,

go freezing by

your eyes are space

one day my heart passed

the knot into a smooth version

in just one day

you and your haunts

were on the subject of the freaky ways

days and violent nights

scent of pain and faded rules April birds fell through May skies

my heart passed

a versatile transmission

fog channel

when I first touched the ground they told me to leave

they were skipping through time

lots of red guys

moving through the grass

but there was more

Tension than that

I believe in a scare with a memory

its been delightful

panoramic vision

spanning the yard

delightful, you pass the store

with your immortal steps

keeping your own descent

here comes my train

here I go, I've got to go, like you, I'll

jump down, I meet someone to believe

see you next June in a memory

picnic, silly

to have passionate

memory see you next week

I believe in a plan with an alley

It got so big it covered the valley

panoramic

Black and white antique

Tamarisk tree, why vegetation

Dust

What are you waiting for

I hear a chorus of sand

angles, you know

triangles

live inside of no day

so somehow it's sad to watch the

standing away

smoke aggravation

could happen to anyone

exception, sweeping

I'm just like everyone

I want to feel the rush of power beneath my wheels

but when I slow I see a ship with sails

competence pulls the stars from the sky west to east

I counted the motions

always a surprise,

you're the

insider inside her

send a letter to Memphis,

let reality read it

process prove it.

WHO HAVE YOU EVER FORGIVEN?

note my weak pinch, EKG, little black moor on road to
recovery from fungus, ? black
on goldy ammonia burn?

midget melon
iron railing

to the windows, outside the day is nice, gracious for   last week of August,
soon it will be time again to read Keats
his odes are barricades
all weather of interest, exciting, then overwhelming

the buildings in it, the design of minds you dwell in mind
when you live in design

except for the sucky renovations, non repairs
like how benny the super (bum) painted a million cat hairs into the bathroom door
which was perfectly fine before.

I'm dreaming of another poetic moment
in a setting entirely different from this one

where I can actually hear these words
without concomitant aggravation

noticed this morning though

early light weakening

shining through a bottle of Sparkle

on windowsill next to noisy fan

the Windermere, Windemere?

—was white-ish, sleepy, a little lazy

DOWN ALONG THE BANKS OF THE WABASH

A feature of this place is its very lateness
landscape riche
pealing church bell, missing cyclist
pizza delivery, stable of ponies,

foggy road
weather,

down along the banks of the Wabash

the rain arrives with a tremendous rush,

concluding another 4th of July. Bombastic
rock and Sousa marches, poor poisoned looking
white people, county courthouse, on the square

I'm sorry, I feel I was so greedy. And mean too.
But remorse won't take the top off this heaviness in my chest, I find.

To me, Indiana is characterized by a beige
vinyl rectangular shape in a green who-knows-what.
people around here love to say hello, that's for sure.

Rip-up clasts waiting to happen
delicate lizard tracks up and down a dune
Beautiful season
brushyfoots fluttering through the Asclepias

Common Yellowthroat, miniscule tadpoles flickering in an ephemeral puddle, a

dragonfly nymph, Voracious

hissing and snapping of electricity

in advance of a freight train:

causes the dinging:

64 cars before you returned with the milk.

Then it was over, the counting part.

The gate went up, and we went up

the hill

Next.

HEADACHE

is it available oxygen controlling

the distribution of algae in

the fishtank?

I woke up with a headache.

WIND IS MY FRIEND

Chicago's wind nips and bites,
then strides right through me
leaving in my place
a pure lighthearted blank.

*

Thank heaven for spiny things
things with edges, stickers, thorns
things that sting, scratch, cause
a rash, scrapes,
needles, spikes
spiny.

*

the chain link oxidized—
hard by a brick wall in January's afternoon

bottle caps dig in
to the asphalt

tattered flag
puffed black plastic grocery bag stuck up in a tree

KLOWN KOLLIDGE

uh uh here it comes
The Scorn

direct from the mouth of a

great big clown

lecturing a class of clowns

NOT acceptable.

righteous indignation
pouring down
like piss

from some clowny high ground

SONG FROM THE ESPERANTO

A hundred bright eyes up in a cypress tree

You are drawing nigh and nigher

Uh Oh my wings are on fire

But just the tips though.

Big angels darken my door

And drop large orbs of music and song

They darken my threshold

And stroke my hands with their antique tongues

They pull my hair

And get my tears to do things.

The silver phone rings. I will answer. Thank you! A gift.

The mystic shape of an antique tongue

Beats my eyes with the grapes of doom.

CANAL OF CONSCIOUSNESS

Hello! I am your American Flag!
I know; hard to believe,
a talking flag.

But you're nothing if not gullible.

Me: waiting for my fries to go at Muskies;
You: Edward Hopper.

You've always wondered about The Rooster Club
and now you find
it's nothing more

than a sandwich.

THE FRUIT OF THE BANANA TREE

He was the only pope they ever knew. He was
quote real unquote.

The portrait is peering straight into you
but in fact it is blind. You, who

never rode the south shore
never went to the pow wow
never kissed Pavlova's slippers

saw the temple burn
entirely missed the harp factory

THE NEW OLD PAINT

Pass the beans Frank
was the last words I heard
before the creosote exploded

I'm not going to Cheyenne
so I'm not leaving Cheyenne

Nonetheless, Just in case
I always find it wise to say
Good bye.

ACKNOWLEDGMENTS

These poems have appeared in the following publications

Ladies Museum, Fresh Paint, The World, Another World, joe soap's canoe, BOMB, Cuz, Little Light, Cover, Shiny, Bridge, Ecstatic Peace, Court Green, Brooklyn Review, Up Is Up, But So Is Down, Poetry Project Newsletter, and *Satellite Telephone*

Thanks to:
City Arts, City of Chicago's Department of Cultural Affairs
Fund for Poetry
Djerassi Foundation
Palenville Interarts
Committee on Poetry

Bob Rosenthal and Rochelle Kraut of Frontward Books
Richard Friedman, Darlene Pearlstein, and Art Lange of Yellow Press
Alex Katz for the cover illustration on the original *Locked from the Outside*
Alice Notley for her wonderful introduction
and Gerald Incandela for the photo on the back cover

Jack Kimball, poet and publisher of Faux/Other

Special Gratitude and Love,

To:

Joshua, Paula, CA, Cathy, Chuck, Peggy, Patti, Marion, Shelley, Jean, Eileen, Ann, and my Mom and Dad